VOCAL SELECTIONS

STOP THE WORLD- I WANT TO GET OFF

MUSIC AND LYRICS BY LESLIE BRICUSSE AND ANTHONY NEWLEY

Ludlow Music, Inc.

TRO The Richmond Organization

LESLIE BRICUSSE

Leslie Bricusse is a writer-composer-lyricist who has contributed to many musical films and plays during his career. The late, great Beatrice Lillie plucked him out of *The Footlights Revue* at the Phoenix Theatre and made him her leading man in *An Evening with Beatrice Lillie* at the Globe Theatre, where he spent the first year of his professional life also writing another musical, *The Boy on the Corner*, and also the screenplay for his first motion picture *Charley Moon*, which won him his first Ivor Novello Award. His subsequent stage musicals include *Stop the World-I Want to Get Off*, *The Roar of the Greasepaint*, *Pickwick*, *Harvey!*, *The Good Old Bad Old Days*, *One Shining Moment* and *Sherlock Holmes-the Musical*.

He has written songs and/or screenplays for such films as *Doctor Dolittle*, *Scrooge*, *Willie Wonka and the Chocolate Factory*, *Goodbye Mr. Chips*, *Victor/Victoria*, *Sunday Lovers*, *Santa Claus*, *Peter Pan* and *The Pied Piper*. Leslie Bricusse has written over thirty musical shows and films, and has collaborated with a *wonderful array of musical talents including* Anthony Newley, Henry Mancini, John Williams, John Barry, Jerry Goldsmith, Jule Styne, Lionel Bart, André Previn and Peter Il-yitch Tchaikovsky (whose *Nutcracker Suite* he adapted into a song score). His better known songs include *What Kind of Fool Am I?*, *Once in a Lifetime*, *Gonna Build a Mountain*, *Who Can I Turn To?*, *The Joker*, *If I Ruled the World*,

My Kind of Girl, *Talk to the Animals*, *You and I*, *Feeling Good*, *When I Look Into Your Eyes*, *Goldfinger*, the love theme from *Superman* (*Can You Read My Mind?*), *You Only Live Twice*, *Le Jazz Hot*, *On a Wonderful Day Like Today*, *Two for the Road* and *The Candy Man*.

He has been nominated for eight Academy Awards, six Grammys, four Tonys, and won two Oscars, a Grammy and seven Ivor Novello Awards, and in 1989 he was inducted into the Songwriters' Hall of Fame. He is currently working on a musical version of *Dr Jekyll and Mr. Hyde* and a Broadway version of *Victor/Victoria*.

ANTHONY NEWLEY

Anthony Newley left school at fourteen. His first film appearance was as The Artful Dodger in David Lean's film of *Oliver Twist*. He wrote four original songs for the film *Idol On Parade* and subsequently created his own revue *Cranks* which was presented at the St. Martin's Theatre and on Broadway.

He wrote *Stop the World-I Want To Get Off* with **Leslie Bricusse** in 1961 and it ran at the Queens Theatre for over a year. Anthony Newley directed it and starred in it. The production was then seen at the Shubert Theater, Broadway where it ran for over 500 performances. In 1964, Anthony Newley and Leslie Bricusse wrote and composed *The Roar Of the Greasepaint-The Smell Of the Crowd* which was presented at the Theatre Royal, Nottingham and subsequently at the Shubert Theater, Broadway. Anthony Newley again directed the productions. In 1972, he directed *The Good Old Bad Old Days* at the Prince of Wales Theatre, again written and composed in conjunction with Leslie Bricusse.

His many film roles include *The Battle of the River Plate, Good Companions, The Small World of Sammy Lee, Dr Dolittle, Sweet November, Can Heironymus Merkin Ever Forget Mercy Humpe and Find True Happiness?* (which he wrote, produced and appeared in), *Willy Wonka and The Chocolate Factory* (Academy Award nomination for the score) and *Mr Quilp* in which he starred and for which he composed the score.

Anthony Newley has appeared in many TV shows on both sides of the Atlantic. He has lived in the USA since 1967. His TV appearances include *The Bill Cosby Special, Cher, Salute To the Beatles,* Anthony Newley Specials, *Golden Globe Awards* and the series *Fame.* He has won gold discs for his compositions *Goldfinger, Candy Man* and *What Kind Of Fool Am I?* His other hit songs include *Who Can I Turn To?, Once In A Lifetime* and *The Man Who Makes You Laugh.* In 1989, Anthony Newley and Leslie Bricusse were inducted into the Songwriters' Hall of Fame in New York.

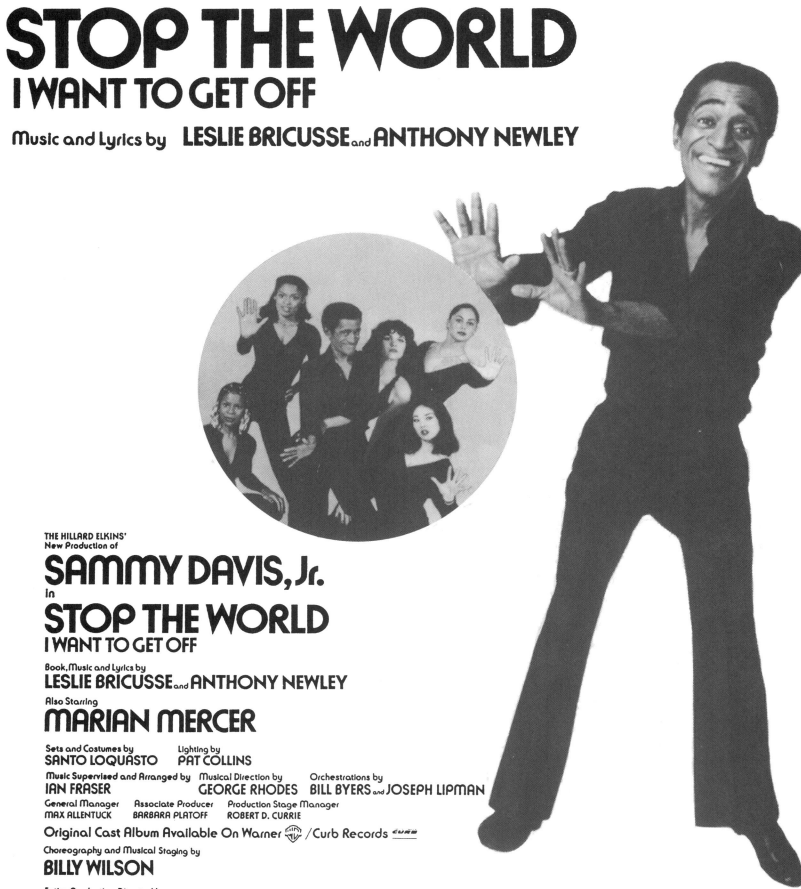

1989 LONDON PRODUCTION

The Production Factory Ltd (Eoin McManus and Bill Denis) & Stan and Sheila Freeman
in association with
The Churchill Theatre, Bromley
by arrangement with Stoll Moss Theatres Ltd
present

ANTHONY NEWLEY
in

STOP THE WORLD
I want to get off

A Musical by
LESLIE BRICUSSE AND ANTHONY NEWLEY
with
RHONDA BURCHMORE
as Evie

and

FIONA ALEXANDA	**KIM ISMAY**
DOLLIE HENRY	**VICTORIA LYNSON**
JULIA HOWSON	**EMMA PRIEST**
SAMANTHA HUGHES	**WENDY SCHOEMANN**

Directed by
ANTHONY NEWLEY

Designed by **DOUGLAS HEAP**	Choreography by **KENN OLDFIELD**	Musical Director **PAUL SMITH**
Lighting Designed by **MARK HENDERSON**	Sound Design by **PHILLIP CLIFFORD**	Orchestrations by **TONY BRITTEN**

Additional Orchestrations by
TERRY DAVIES & IAN FRAZER

from the Broadway production "STOP THE WORLD—I WANT TO GET OFF"

I WANNA BE RICH

Words and Music by
LESLIE BRICUSSE & ANTHONY NEWLEY

7

Lyrics from the 1978 production:

I wanna be rich with money to burn,
About ten grand a week, say, is what I oughta earn,
I'd keep it in bundles in case of a slump,
I would spread largesse and the I.R.S.
Could take a running jump.
I'd have all my suits made — a dozen a time,
I'd buy all the best shares providing they climb,
Give me half a chance and a small advance, my fingers itch
To make me dirty rotten filthy stinking rich.

I wanna be rich and live in L.A.,
Go crazy at nighttime and sleep in the day,
An Italian car as long as the street,
And the local broads will arrive in hordes,
It'll knock 'em off their feet.
I wanna be famous and be in the news,
And date a t.v. star whenever I choose,
Give me half a chance to lead a dance and make my pitch
And I'll be dirty rotten filthy stinking rich.

I wanna be rich and mix with the nobs,
And sit in the best seats with all of the snobs,
I may go to Ascot to take in the scene,
In my grey top hat and my spats and that,
I'd be comp'ny for the Queen.
I wanna go trav'ling to Cannes and Capri,
The French Riviera is my cup of tea;
Give me half a chance in the south of France with some rich bitch
And I'll be dirty rotten filthy stinking,
Hear the silver dollars clinking,
Lots of broads and lots of drinking,
I can guess what you're all thinking,
Dirty rotten filthy stinking rich.

from the Broadway production "STOP THE WORLD—I WANT TO GET OFF"

TYPICALLY ENGLISH

Words and Music by
LESLIE BRICUSSE & ANTHONY NEWLEY

pa - tience while the Ty - pic - 'lly Eng - lish rain is pour - ing down. ___
vanc - es though I'm bound to con - fess I find them rath - er nice. ___

We've a Ty - pic - 'lly Eng - lish span - iel who likes Ty - pic - 'lly Eng - lish walks past the
In the Ty - pic - 'lly Eng - lish sum - mer we take Ty - pic - 'lly Eng - lish trips to a

Ty - pic - 'lly Eng - lish trees up - on the heath. And if an - y - one asks me
ty - pic - 'lly sea - side place with Aunt - ie Maude. And if an - y - one asks me

how I like this Ty - pic - 'lly Eng - lish life, I am fed up to my Ty - pic - 'lly Eng - lish
how I like this Ty - pic - 'lly Eng - lish life, I have nev - er been

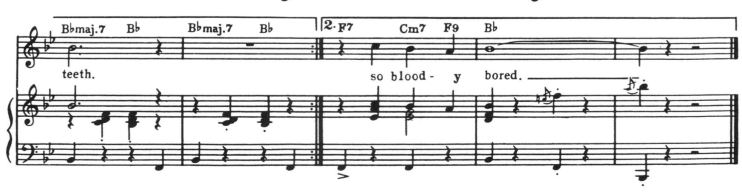

teeth.   so blood - y bored. ___

Note: the following lyrics are sung to the same music as
"Typically English"

GLORIOUS RUSSIAN

My mother said I never should
Mix with subversive, reactionary elements in the wood.
If I did, she would say,
You'll only end up as a decadent, subservient
Western, imperialistic, political
Puppet one day.

I'm a glorious Russian comrade
Born on glorious Russian soil,
I was part of my glorious
Parents' five year plan.
I eat glorious Russian salad
That's imported from the West,
And drink glorious Russian
Vodka when I can.

I've got fourteen glorious brothers
Down a glorious Russian mine,
I've got fifteen glorious
Sisters and a cat.
And the lot of us live together
In such glorious Russian bliss,
In a glorious Soviet
Russian two-room flat.

Father is a glorious Russian postman,
Mother drives a glorious Russian tram.
Grandma drives a tractor though she's ninety-four,
And Grandpa doesn't give a Russian damn.

We've got glorious Russian writers
Locked in glorious Russian jails,
And the glorious Russian
News says one fine day:
We'll live happily ever after
On a vast collective farm
Somewhere in the glorious
Soviet U.S.A.

TYPISCHE DEUTSCHE

Der Vaterland said I never should
Play mit anyone in the wood.
That would only mean disgrace,
We'd never end up as the Master Race.

I'm a typische Deutsche fräulein
Born of typische Deutsche stock,
With a typische Deutsche
Fräulein's point of view.
I eat typische Deutsche sauerkraut
Und drink typische Deutsche beer,
Und mein typische Deutsche
Dachshund drinks it too.

I love typische Deutsche music
Played by typische Deutsche bands,
As we dance beneath a
Typische Deutsche moon.
Though I love the songs of Schubert
Und the melodies of Brahms,
Deutschland Uber Alles
Ist my fav'rite tune.

Vater ist ein typische Deutsche doctor,
But he was a general in the war,
He still keeps his uniform in the cupboard,
Just in case we should see the day he's waiting for.

We are typische Deutsche people,
We have typische Deutsche ways,
Und a typische Deutsche
Outlook on the world.
Und on Adolf Hitler's birthday
In our sentimental way,
How we love to see our
Dear old flag unfurled.
Happy Birthday, dear Adolf,
Wherever you are.

ALL-AMERICAN

My mother said, "Don't screw around."
Based on experience I have found
If I did, she would say,
"You'll only be sorry on Labor Day."

I'm an all-American beauty
Selling all-American dreams,
They're the kind Horatio
Alger said come true;
I'm a glittering example
Of democracy at work,
I'm an all-American
Irish Polish Jew.

I'm an all-American symbol
Of executive success
From stenographer to
Corporate lady whiz;
Anybody can be President
Of these great United States,
And to prove it,
Almost anybody is!

Daddy couldn't utter a word of English,
But he became the multiest millionaire;
Mummy and I are proud of Daddy's porno shops,
His all-American dream was planted there.

There is only one thing missing
From my all-American life,
That's a man who'll make our
Marriage his career;
He will learn to cook and clean for me
And drive me home from work
In an all-American car
That lasts a year.

Since first I went to college,
People saw what I could be,
The football players voted me
Miss Touchdown Sixty-three;
Since then I've had to fight the fight
For women's liberty,
So here comes Lorene,
I'm as clean as chlorine,
Liberty-lovin' Lorene,
That's me!

Words and Music by LESLIE BRICUSSE and ANTHONY NEWLEY

from the Broadway production "STOP THE WORLD—I WANT TO GET OFF"

LUMBERED

Words and Music by
LESLIE BRICUSSE & ANTHONY NEWLEY

Lyrics from the 1978 production:

I've been L.U.M.B.E.R.E.D. lumbered,
And I can't pretend I find it any fun,
I'm too young to be a father,
There are lots of things I'd rather be,
And trust me, being lumbered isn't one.
When I ought to be completely unencumbered,
I've been forced to buy a ring and say Amen,
I've been L.U.M.B.E.R.E.D. lumbered but!
I'm never gonna get lumbered again.

I've been L.U.M.B.E.R.E.D. lumbered,
And I gotta say I'm feeling pretty choked,
Bang go all my lovely visions,
I've been forced to make decisions,
Wish I had a dime for every pack I've smoked.
When I think of all the chicks with whom I've slumbered,
Now I'll only ever see them now and then,
I've been L.U.M.B.E.R.E.D. lumbered but!
I'm never gonna get lumbered again.

If I ever get my hands upon the idiot who wrote,
Into ev'ry life a little rain must fall,
I shall take his book of wisdom
And I'll shove it up his throat,
Little rain, my ass, I seem to get it all.

I've been L.U.M.B.E.R.E.D. lumbered,
It's enough to drive a fellow M.A.D.
I am scarcely past my childhood,
I still play the games a child would,
I'm still playing Moms and Dads as you can see.
When I think of all the chicks with whom I've rhumbaed,
For the wedding march I'm lumbered with a hen,
I've been quite unduly well and truly lumbered but!
I'm never gonna get lumbered again.

from the Broadway production "STOP THE WORLD—I WANT TO GET OFF"

GONNA BUILD A MOUNTAIN

Words and Music by
LESLIE BRICUSSE and ANTHONY NEWLEY

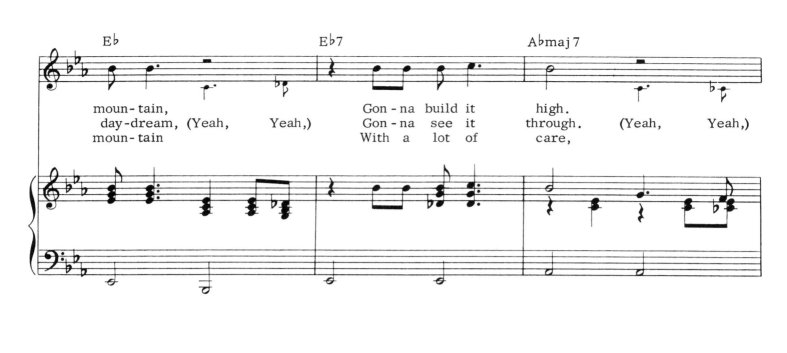

moun-tain,
day-dream, (Yeah, Yeah,)
moun-tain

Gon-na build it high.
Gon-na see it through. (Yeah, Yeah,)
With a lot of care,

I don't know how I'm gon-na do it, on-ly know I'm gon-na
Gon-na build a moun-tain and a day-dream, gon-na make 'em both come
And take my day-dream up the moun-tain, heav-en will be wait-ing

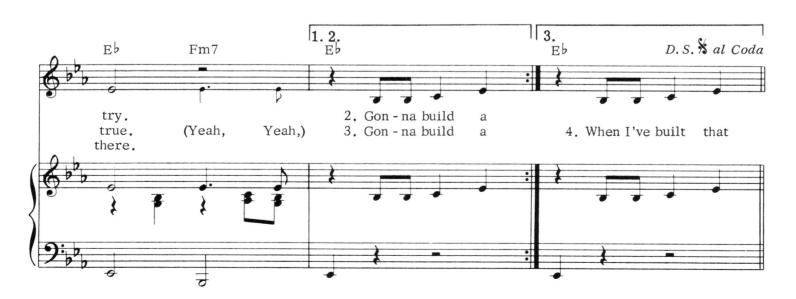

try.
true. (Yeah, Yeah,)
there.

2. Gon-na build a
3. Gon-na build a

4. When I've built that

from the Broadway production "STOP THE WORLD—I WANT TO GET OFF"

MEILINKI MEILCHIK

Words and Music by
LESLIE BRICUSSE & ANTHONY NEWLEY

from the Broadway production "STOP THE WORLD—I WANT TO GET OFF"

ONCE IN A LIFETIME

Words and Music by
LESLIE BRICUSSE & ANTHONY NEWLEY

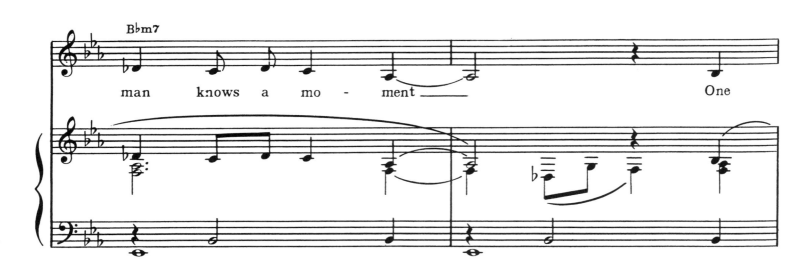

SOMEONE NICE LIKE YOU

Words and Music by
LESLIE BRICUSSE & ANTHONY NEWLEY

from the Broadway production "STOP THE WORLD—I WANT TO GET OFF"

WHAT KIND OF FOOL AM I?

Words and Music by
LESLIE BRICUSSE and ANTHONY NEWLEY

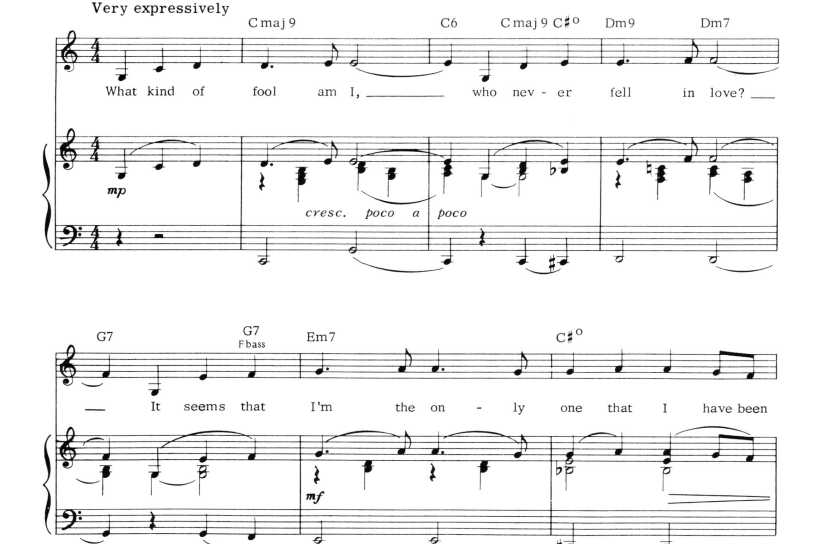